CW01090765

What is This?

A Conversation
Between
10 Poets

Table of Contents

An Invitation

When I first read my poem (the first one in this book) during a session with a critique group, my fellow poets began to discuss their answers to the question posed in the last line "what is this?" After one of them asked if he could *write* a response to the question, the idea of this collection was born.

Nine poets from different parts of the country have taken part by creating seventeen unique answers in poetry form. The result is a revealing conversation, one we are pleased to share with you. It is our wish you too will experience the freedom to interpret poetry through *your* way of looking at the world.

Now—come join the conversation.

Gaea Bailey

A Poem by Gaea Bailey ⇨

you only write it
on the walls of the temple
in splashes of color that
can be seen as far away
      as yesterday.

it can only be read
with eyes cemented
in the poverty between
confrontation
      and sin

only washed away by
laughter of children
as brightest lights of day
give way to clouds of
      memory

scribed in darkly morn
      captured again

i ask the holy seven
      what is this?

Poems by Barbara Whitesides Peña ⇨

under the dark mists of time and secrecy
I open the histories of man
and proclaim

they came with tools
the aboriginals, the spiritualists, the artists,
                                    and the vandals
to scratch and paint and tattoo
    on boulders of granite
    walls and canyons of sandstone
    stuccoed concrete structures of rebar
    and the skins of buffalos and men
for they are always driven to record life
on these sacred spaces of truth

colored in shades of blood clans
the tinting tales of battles and hunts
bubbled letterings marking territories
and emblazoned glories of artistic creation
all calling to be seen and remembered and honored

these spaces of worship are owned
                        by those who stake their claim
for they drive the stake deep into others' souls
where faith grows tall and strong

sometimes rains may wash away their visions
                              of strength and conquest
                              of beauty
                              of pain and sorrow
those who have created and witnessed the elemental
                                        desecration
seek no forgiveness or mercy
for they feel the presence and essence of mankind
they hear the echoes of so many voices

            so, when you ask the holy seven
            what is this?

            this is the single eternal cry of man

                I WAS HERE

on the outskirts of her mind
she frescoes distant memories
in reds and blacks
smeared in blurred grays

written there, so deep, lie secrets of her life's
desperation and wantings
her search for The Self
buried in sealed copper coffins
silent echoes of prior deeds
kept hidden from sour judgements and eyes confronting

she seeks redemption
a spiritual reborning and
to walk into those thin places
where grace meets forgiveness
to be heard in the giggling mouths of children

those passions of youth
illustrated on mindscreens
are moving shadows now
wearing the shrouds of grief and remorse

never will they speak
the holy language of angels
for they are not of heaven

A Poem by Kit Boyer ⇨

in the eyes of the comaschi youth

we stare across the sea
at a future eaten by the gods
a present stayed

first came the cloud
glowing wrapping
within which
many fingers played
many voices sung

and our stories too
are there
carved on faces
written on walls
by Eros Lyssa Pothos
Nike Euphrosyne
and all the small gods
of every house

hands hold one another
through flash and heat
flesh and ash and hollow
and plaster
and what is suspended
in the folds of time
mother and babe
maid and charge
master and thief

we cast now
the small teeth
and learn of storgē
see ourselves in
the delicate arch of arms
the laying of hem to lips

and Hypnos danced with
Mnemosyne
until their feet bled
and their smiles fell
and they lay together trembling
over all of it
unto
the great dark

only Soteina could not be found

*A Poem by Jasen Thompson
aka Orion 3.6.9.* ⇨

This is

This is the point where the whirling wind sweeps up the trees and prevailing wind sweeps the seas into whirlwind drowning everything below it and sucking everything above it down to its proverbial knees begging it to breathe life into the dead eyes it sees it dying from the disease that light then cures but in that moment the bullet strikes an artery that God holds his finger on my pulse as I reach my outstretched hand for the demons to pull me way from clutches of their brethren
This is
    Stopping me from
      Remembering all that kills me
       Strengthens the monsters or
Shield me. angels are the moments where the cold is chilling enough to numb but not to bone where the breath whispers from the greys don't go hollow as those breaths go wisping past the flickering light threatening to go dim but somehow finds kindling forever giving hope whether it is wanted or not.
Why can't. . . I have the power to discern when wisdom is earned so the question still remains
What is this?

Poems by Bob Blatz ⇨

19

Mothering with a Capital "S"

Perugino, stop splashing
or you'll get a time out.

Put down that trowel,
you'll poke an eye out.

Wipe that smile off your face
it's no laughing matter.

You're trying my patience.
Get down off that ladder.

On Parenting

If you name your child
Sandalphon,
he had better become
an archangel.

Poems by Ien Nivens ⇨

what it is.

          i call it sometimes   not quite mockingly but
          with a sense of bewilderment is more
          is more like it   gibberish i call it but i still
          still let myself do it speak in tongues it's
                                        it's a drug
                  a pure white powder.

          and yet   and yet   i don't *believe* in it
          like i'm supposed to   that it's angel language
          or one of the ones we spoke when babel fell
          that the holy ghost lights me like a candle
                  moves me by the tongue

          still   light fills me like a freshfallen child in love
          with the mystery of   christ, well   existence
          the utter plenitude of being   and of
          all the happenstances of science   and in fact it
                  it does me no great harm

          to mutter it now and again
                  when i'm alone

          i'd ask the holy spirit
              what it is.

this old thing?

just a keepsake
from the old northside assembly
picture the bride with her skirts in the wind
like blossompetals whished as far away
                as yes

today i tilt my head
adjust my spectacles
and sightread the lines between
conjugation
                and sin

awash in the laughter of two disruptive brothers
who got the daylights beaten out of them
after the reception
david's dad twisterwhipping his belt
                was a sight to remember

but memory's brittle
                as a dated polaroid

fifty-seven years old
                this old thing.

this is it.

      this wedding of word to word
      we do
      in binding black and white
      fingerweaving on a bible
        forever and a day (.)

      this inscrutable moment
      this concretion of eventualities
      cementing the meum and the tuum
      in public accord
            in the sanctioned sin

      of temple violation   and the theft of a half-life
      to make one laughing whole
      of prism-splintered light
      behind the teardrenched eye
          of here and now

      this scribbling in sequestered dark
          we do together   alone

      with the trust of the newly wed
        this is it.

what barb read.

in a cathedral
under the highway
a hooded priest performs
a neon sacrament
in ultraviolet night.

his gibberish is encoded
in blemished concrete
that seamripped the city
to contain
the crime

of a white panel truck parked
under the viaduct
while men in hazmat suits
whitewash
the blasphemy away

it bleeds through   though
if you catch the sunrise right

i think you can still make out
what barb read.

this marking time.

       your name inscribed
       on the wall   at the temple
       in the lobby
       on a parallelogrammatic splash
             of brass.

       we say it aloud
       at your yahrzeit
       standing   looking faraway
       where the colors of yesterday
             have faded

       we wash you down like wine
       with the laughter of wistfulness
       and a sparkle in the eye
       making room for each other
             in memoriam

       this is the magic
             of dittography

       this marking time
             together.

who is she?

she only visits the temple
when she wants
to make a splash
like a mermaid on the horizon
        of far ago.

take a telescoping lens   scry for her
with an eye fixed
on the poverty between
imagination
        and sin

she vanishes
in a spray of laughter
spangled all the brighter
for the pewter cloudbank
        backdropping her

scribbled in its turn on red dusk
        and released again

to the seven seas
        who *is* she?

in here.

mom warned me
my body's a temple
don't defile it
reason people lived eight hundred years
        in the bible?

she theorized
they ate better
on what the lord provided
than what we get nowadays
        at the grocery

jesus washed away nine tenths
of my childhood
i chased his light so hard
it blinded me
        on the inside

made it harder to read
        the scripture scribbled

seven layers deep
        in here

A Poem by Michael D. Huff ⇨

Untitled Response

My sight

Is embedded in your eyes

For life gives challenges

To make me fight

Against the enemy lines

Strength is enclosed

In the flesh

Of my soul

Weakness is mental

For darkness

To explode

Forgive me of my sins

When being damned by four

I want to be blessed

By two

If not more

Struggles of life

Breaks me

To be unstable

In poverty, bare

Chilled to the core

Spare change to clothe

Irony of being the once ignored

In the jungle of possibilities

Being prey

However be

The missing key

Of what is

Being different

Or becoming the same

To reject

My invitations

This must be my light

Peeking through the darkness

With child laughter of joyous play

Filling my heart with slight glimmer

Of happiness and love

This question they ask me

Upon being blessed with talent

To spread a message

This is my response

Let me be

The second letter

Of the alphabet

To heal my wounds

Of sin and condonement

A poem by Benjamin McClellan ⇨

Bags of Bones (A Response to 'What is this')

A bag of bones lays undisturbed in the dust
buried for thousands of years it lay
in a time forgotten, an eon without mercy
the tales they tell are a mystery
of wars and conflict seeming
a part of humanity's struggle with itself

Curiously they lay dormant yet full
of things cast randomly around them
a sword   a shield   a helmet of bronze
fragments of cloth with tiny bits
sewn to show the worth of the owners
who no longer need the recognition

We examine closely these bits and pieces
discover their importance to history
realizing strife has always existed
power vacuums filled in by the powerful
slaves and the poor forced to kill
all for the price of   a sword a shield and a helmet

"Tale as old as time," to borrow a phrase
from an era where the wealthy powerful
could order the killing of thousands—hasn't
changed much
all in the name of greed of polity of narcissism
while the conquered wailed in anguish
at the loss of friends and family

You would think we were over this
love mercy compassion   charity prevailing
you would be wrong replaced with missiles and bullets
innocents murdered daily, houses and buildings
crumble like so much feta cheese
a dish all the more humbling because

we are selfish
        we are greedy
                    we hold grudges
                        we seek revenge
                                    we hold terror at our fingertips

this is such a time as the bags of bones
tell the story

A poem by Yvette Saenz ⇨

What Is This?

The sign on the wall of the flower shop at Safeway reads
Poetry in Bloom. Always be aware of the location of the nearest exit.
Have faith in the hidden workings of Providence.
God says: I never make a mistake. God requests my service,
my friendship. Tells me to depart, run away,
and never return. For the good of my homeland.
Anyway, it's no longer home. I must act accordingly,
because death is in the checkout line at Safeway
between a woman who has saved $90 on a $70 order
and a man with an FBI cap, I'm very sure he doesn't work for
the FBI, and a young woman across the counter who makes
$12 an hour to put up with this shit, and I am thinking
the only cushion between myself and death is —
Nothing. There is no cushion. I lie to myself
that I am a lucky one. They called us gifted & talented in
elementary. To separate the part from the whole. I am much
sicker, my heart in the wrong place. It's a spy, an enigma.
Everything she says is a lie.
You and me both. I don't need anyone
to teach me to survive is to lie. Another lie:
I only believe the people who love me. I never believe them.
Another: I can't stop this killing. And still — everything
changes around me,
bread always two steps ahead. I feign like I don't know
what this is. Greedy - that's what makes us alike.
Me and my heart
pretending to cry over spilled milk as if someone didn't spill
the milk on purpose so that we'd cry instead of demanding
a life that doesn't kill. I didn't get my sane dream.

My sane dream = I respectfully decline
this march into madness. Everyone is buying t-shirts
with names. Not their own. Drink our Logos
as I kill milk. No reason to get so emotional about my lack
of imagination, about the tangerines, grapes, strawberries
rolling away on the pavement.

Beauty doesn't belong here.
I can't not see the beauty.
Wouldn't I like to live, have sex, write
as if I held the universe in my hands?

A poem by Randy Sproat ⇨

What this is

who has eyes to see
letters from a language
with only a single surviving reader?
if green is the sharpest color, the past
is written in viridian
hidden in the holiest
of holies

but all the blinded Basils
of history are but stones within a falling wall,
woven reed-work, built to burn
the ancient things we only remember
from our sleep

if it had a voice to cry
the drawstring was long ago pulled tight
perhaps it comes around, circling,
a plutonic-return, black-winged
perhaps it is only us spinning

never learning
what this is

Meet the Poets ⇨

Gaea Bailey

Gaea found new life in her poetry in recent years after decades of writing for academia and businesses in Arizona. Born in upstate New York, she was fortunate to attend a regional public high school that offered advanced courses in all fields. She was drawn to the art of poetry in her writing courses. During the recent worldwide gap in the bustle of life, she was reminded of her love for writing and returned to poetry forms she had left behind. Gaea has also found a new joy in performing her poetry at venues throughout the Phoenix area. Her work has been published by Moonstone Press, Phoenix Oasis Press and others. Old Hunt Road Press is her latest endeavor. It is a small press designed to bring poetry to the public in imaginative ways. A collection of her poems *An Afternoon of Perspicacity*, is planned to be released during 2025. Gaea welcomes comments and questions at oldhuntroadpress@yahoo.com

Bob Blatz

Bob is working toward a creative writing certificate at Mesa Community College where he has been teaching Child & Family Studies and Education courses since 2007.

Bob and his wife, Linda, are compiling a collection of letters, poetic rants, and snide attacks on the universe following the death of their daughter, Margot, from an overdose.

Kit Boyer

Kit Boyer is a writer. She recently published a poetry chapbook titled *Echo* with the assistance of a local arts grant. She's written serialized fiction, hosted a writing podcast, worked as an editor, and facilitated several in-person and online writing critique groups. Kit believes in a thing called love.

Michael D. Huff

My name is Michael D. Huff. Writing gives me a chance for my love of storytelling and imagination to take life. I recently published *For The Love I Found*, a story about a young woman finding love within her best friend. It is a story that truly moves one with the power and acceptance of love. It is available on Amazon.

Benjamin McClellan

Retired music teacher of 25 years, musician and poet. Recently published a new book titled Regaining Belief*: A Personal Medicine Collective*, available on Amazon.

Ien Nivens

An artist and educator by training and a poet/novelist by inclination, Ien Nivens grew up on the pentecostal plains of Oklahoma. He currently lives in Mesa, Arizona, with his wife, the quilt artist Michelle Jensen, Kirby, aka Best Dog Ever, and a feline terrorist known as Jalepeno.

Mr. Nivens is the author of *The American Book of Changes*, a re-interpretation and reinvigoration of the 64 hexagrams of the classic Chinese divination system known as the I Ching. *Tangible Angels* is his first novel. He is currently working on a fantasy series about a disfigured princess and her portraitist.

Yvette Saenz

I am a writer from Alice, Texas. I live in Tucson, where I'm a graduate student in the Master of Fine Arts Program in Creative Writing at University of Arizona. My first chapbook of poems *South Texas Starry Night* (Shut Eye Press) will be available for purchase sometime in late 2024-early 2025. The book is my narrative poetry about growing up in an oilfield town in rural South Texas in a family full of chaos, love, and art, then attending Harvard University and experiencing extreme culture shock, and finally understanding my family's dark history and accepting myself via my interaction with the visual art of Vincent Van Gogh. I am currently working on a creative non-fiction book tentatively titled *Van Gogh's Women*. To purchase a copy of my chapbook or for other book/writing related questions or comments, email me at ysaenzwrites@gmail.com.

Randy Sproat

Randy has lived in Arizona his entire life. He has been writing poetry since kindergarten. He has hosted in-person and online poetry critiques in the Phoenix Metro area and continues to write and share his own work.

Jasen Randall Thompson

I wrote my first poem at the age of 13. That poem was selected for a statewide competition. I served in the Marine Corps during which I occasionally competed in poetry competitions. I am father of two adults and have been a member of the Red Sands community for about 2 years.

Barbara Whitesides Peña

My love of creative writing was born when I was very young. My daddy, a WWII veteran and ex-prisoner of war, loved the beauty of the English language. He lovingly corrected my words, both spoken and written, and that of my two sisters, because he knew the power of its usage. He quoted Shakespearean soliloquies when occasions arose for their appropriate use. He set the standard that has driven my appreciation and passion for the perfect word and its perfect placement.

I was born and spent the first twenty-three years of my life in South Louisiana. The beauty and lushness of that environment and the creatures that inhabit the swamps and bayous fill my thoughts and dreams. Although I live in the desert Southwest, I continue to be deeply influenced by the waters and peoples who call that world their home.

I began composing poetry forty years ago when I was working on a university degree. In the last five years I began anew when I was encouraged to create by my friend and mentor, Dr. Marythelma Brainard Ransom. I am immeasurably grateful to her and to my husband, Stan, who supports me in all I do. While these are my first poems in print, I am working toward a personal collection to be published soon.